Don & Annette,
I'd like to write another poem,
but my feeble brain
so if you'd like a b___
read the other on
still me!
John Metzig

Don & Annette
These past two
years have been very
enjoyable. Your
friendship has
been very valuable
to me. — Glenn Schultz

SPILLED MILK

SPILLED MILK
Litanies for Living

KAY SMALLZRIED

New York   Oxford University Press   1964

The quotations from St. Paul's Letter to the Corinthians I, Chapter 13, are from *The New English Bible,* © the Delegates of the Oxford University Press and the Syndics of the Cambridge University Press, 1961, and are reprinted by permission.

PREFACE

The litanies in this book were written over a three-year period and half of them have been used either publicly, privately, or both.

Many friends encouraged me and suggested subjects.

I wish particularly to acknowledge my indebtedness to the following: the Reverend G. Clayton Melling and Jessie Melling; Marion Pelton, who gave valuable assistance in the preparation of the manuscript; Barbara Cant, Margery Follansbee, Mary Gill, Selma Marquard, Virginia Robbins, Kay Tank, and Fanny Walker.

Mamaroneck, N. Y.   KAY SMALLZRIED
September, 1963

CONTENTS

PART III

THE SEVEN AGES OF MAN

PART IV

CRISIS

PART V

THE SEVEN CAPITAL SINS

SPILLED MILK

The Use of Litanies

Litany comes from the Greek word meaning prayer. In English the word refers to a particular kind of worship, the *invocations, petitions, entreaties* said by the minister, or group leader, with *responses* said by the congregation, or group.

In the following litanies the sentences printed in *italics* are the *responses*.

Litanies are, of course, often used as private devotions, as well as in church services, by prayer groups, in retreats or quiet days, and at youth conferences.

PART I

ATTITUDES OF MIND

1 ‖ Of Spilled Milk

Sacred Trinity, One God,
Known in stillness,
Hear our prayers.

Be still, and know that You are God?
But this wretched accident!
This milk must be mopped up,
Broken glass swept away,
The children gotten off to school,
Shirts ironed,
Letters written,
Meetings attended,
Bills paid,
Telephoning done,
Be still, You say?
Lord, know our situation.

Be still and know that You are God?
There's money to be borrowed,
Planes caught,
Contracts written,
Transactions completed,
Machines invented,
Men fired,
Men hired,

Reports written,
Reports read,
Conferences planned,
Tomorrow anticipated
In today.
Be still, You say?
Lord, know our situation.

Be still and know that You are God?
There are jobs to be looked for,
Rights to be fought for,
Respect to be earned,
Dignity to be achieved,
The humanity of all,
Lord,
To be made beautiful.
Be still, You say?
Lord, know our situation.

You know all this.
But some nagging insecurity within us
Urges that we meet
Your authority
With explanation of ourselves:
For ourselves, perhaps,
And not for You.
Yes, Lord, once we know that You have heard us
In our terms and not in history's,
We shall be still
And listen for Your voice.
Lord, know our situation.

2 || Of Grace

God the Father,
God the Son,
God the Holy Spirit,
Most Glorious Trinity, One God,
Be with us now.

When we, in nights of pain, dismay, and grief,
In torment of mind, confusion, and despair,
Take flight within ourselves to hide from You,
Come, Holy Spirit, and fill us with Your grace.

When we forsake decision, strength, and peace,
Forsake Your costly joy for cheaper pleasure,
And drift directionless upon the world,
Come, Holy Spirit, and fill us with Your Grace.

When we, at odds with life, with death,
With home, with friend, with place, with self,
At odds with everlastingness,
Seek refuge in the meaningless,
Come, Holy Spirit, and fill us with Your grace.

When we have reached our undeserving worst,
And jeopardized our souls with lethargy,
Submitting to dull habit's tyranny,
Come, Holy Spirit, and fill us with Your grace.

Scrape clean our minds,
That we may think of You,
Unveil our eyes,
That we may see You,
Quicken our hearts,
That we may serve You,
Form our desires,
That we may suit You.

The journey to redemption is begun,
Surrendered to You, we shall try to go
Wherever You ask us,
Knowing that on the way we shall meet,
Must meet,
Your Cross.
Come, Holy Spirit, and fill us with Your grace.

3 ‖ Of Doubt

Blessed Trinity, One God,
Essence of Eternity,
Teach us gratitude.

At times when we are filled with doubt,
Doubt You, or miracles, or truth,
And our soul's needs are heavy, arid, tired,
Lord, teach us gratitude.

If no prayer fits our lips, no praise
Fills our hearts, no song lifts our minds,
And all our searching for You finds us lost,
Lord, teach us gratitude.

Though our ambitions lie in ashes,
Our efforts vanished in disappointment,
Our identity gone in all we tried to do,
Lord, teach us gratitude.

Because in such times as these,
We shall learn that
"Faith is the substance of things hoped for,
The evidence of things not seen."
Lord, teach us gratitude.

4 || Of Simple Significance

O Blessed Trinity,
O Holy Mystery, One God,
Set us free.

When our lives are chained
To insignificance,
How shall we move into
Your Loving Light?
We beseech You, Lord, set us free.

When our love is chained
To selfishness,
How shall we ever know
The gallantry of
Your gay Selflessness?
We beseech You, Lord, set us free.

When our minds are chained
To thoughtlessness,
How shall we escape
To the bright spontaneity
Of Your Eternity?
We beseech You, Lord, set us free.

When our souls are chained
To pettiness,
How shall we liberate them
To Your Joyous Peace?
We beseech You, Lord, set us free.

Preserve us,
God,
From lives
Of sinful
Insignificance.
We beseech You, Lord, set us free.

5 || Of Salvation

Blessed Trinity, One God,
Source of our Salvation,
Have mercy upon us.

On days when Your Commandment is unwelcome,
And, feeling ourselves unloved, we pass the hours
Idolizing our inconsequence,
Lord, spur us to salvation.

At times, when You, Your love, seem so remote
Because we close our eyes to all You give,
Forsaking the reality of spirit
For transient tangibility,
Lord, spur us to salvation.

How difficult it is to love ourselves
And know that in self-love we bring to You
Some worship of the gifts You bring to us,
And then to turn
Our thoughts, our lives, our substance
To the world
That all may join
Your praise
Imperishable.
Lord, spur us to salvation.

6 || Of Thankfulness

Triumphant Trinity, One God,
Generous of Joy,
Accept our thanks.

On days of gladness when, with grateful hearts,
We prize life's multitude of gifts,
Lord, accept our thanks.

For the fun of hearing music, laughter, bird-song,
family voices, spring rain, surf-crash, dry leaves,
squeaking snow, street sounds, friendly greetings,
fireplace logs, good conversation, new ideas, machinery,
jazz drums, summer insects, base-hits, stadium cheers,
card shuffles, church bells, hymns, and prayers,
For all the self-forgetful moments our ears have brought to us,
Lord, accept our thanks.

For the glow of seeing ballet, rainbows, water-lilies,
moonlight, athletes, ancient sculpture, modern painting,
skyscrapers, canyons, children Christmas morning,
spring bloodroot, summer roses, autumn maples,
winter landscape, dawn-lit mountain tops, spiral galaxies,
living cells, friendly smiles, fresh-turned earth,
skilled performance, love's health, city lights,
deft needlework, ocean tides,
church spires, sun-married stained glass windows,
and Your flower-decorated altar,
For all the self-forgetful moments our eyes have caught for us,
Lord, accept our thanks.

For the cheer of feeling clean sheets, earned rest,
morning dew, first frost, thawing breeze, good golf swings,
saddle-horses, tennis strokes, swimming power, full sails,
relaxed muscles, hot baths, achievement, excitement,
a child's kiss, a friendly embrace, ourselves expressed,
For the grace of Your cup against our lips,
For all the self-forgetful moments our touch has reached for us,
Lord, accept our thanks.

For the treat of tasting winter asparagus, spring lamb,
summer strawberries, autumn pumpkin pies, birthday cakes,

9

friendly toasts, hot coffee, crisp salad, fresh crackers,
aged cheese, church suppers, ice-cream, picnics, roast beef,
family breakfasts, social luncheons, dinner out,
midnight snacks,
For the redeeming Joy of Your sacred feast,
For all the self-forgetful moments our taste has savored for us,
Lord, accept our thanks.

For the zest of scenting onions in the stew, hickory smoke,
spring lilacs, summer salt air, autumn bonfires, winter furs,
enchanting perfume, chilled melons, fresh-cut limes,
a new-bathed infant, good wine, rain-soaked earth, hot bread,
jelly-making, cake-spice, oil paint, rubbed sage,
waxed wood, soft leather,
The gentle, benediction-fragrance of the candles on Your altar,
For all the self-forgetful moments our breathing discovers for us,
Lord, accept our thanks.

In all we do, Lord,
Help us to find
Beauty for ashes,
The oil of joy for mourning,
The garments of praise
For the spirit of heaviness,
And then,
Lord, accept our thanks.

7 ‖ Of Manifestation

Father, Son, Holy Spirit,
Mystery made manifest, One God,
Have mercy upon us.

If You give Your unsearchable riches to us
Only to find
We happily cling
To the counterfeit treasures of this world,
Lord, be patient with us.

If You must see in us
That riches are such things as we can count,
And touch, and feel, and own,
While we must learn from You
A wealth named truth
Inherited through pain,
Lord, be patient with us.

If You should find us small, afraid, and hidden
Behind the clutter of things we schemed to get,
Lord, be patient with us.

If we need time to turn away from wants
And know Your gifts
As we know food and bed,
Lord, be patient with us.

And if, in the turmoil of our thoughts,
We sense at last the act You have performed,
Committing Yourself to us, inviting us to bring ourselves to You,
Lord, keep us in that faith.

For in Your redeeming love
You are manifest to us,
And we, Your frail and dusty images,
Become alive to You.

Lord, have mercy upon us.
Christ, have mercy upon us.
Lord, have mercy upon us.

8 ‖ Of Spiritual Growth

Holy Trinity,
Mystery manifest in love, One God,
Enlarge our spirit.

If clear perception and the power to act
Conflict with our desire or lazy habit,
Lord, enlarge our spirit.

If we give the name of right
To what we want,
Or smother Your emerging Kingdom
In eiderdown conformity.
Lord, enlarge our spirit.

If we avoid decisions as though they were a curse,
And stifle Your creative love
In some bewildering agony
Of frustrating sentimentality,
Lord, enlarge our spirit.

If we fear to be transformed from what we are
To what You planned for us from the beginning,
If we complicate Your grace
With selfish longings,
Lord, enlarge our spirit.

Lord,
Let our spirit be measured
By the vivid wisdom
Of Your simplicity,
Fill our spirit with the
Courage of our redemption,

Release our spirit
To Your service,
And then,
To meet the needs of others,
Lord, enlarge our spirit, once again.

9 ‖ Of Frailty

Existing Trinity, One God,
Creating force of eternity,
Help us to be strong.

Because our faith is frail,
And, wise in our own conceits,
We try to solve our problems alone,
Lord, save us from ourselves.

Because our perseverance sags,
And, pressed by our desires,
We choose some random folly
Rather than wait for what You would have us do,
Lord, save us from ourselves.

Because our fears imprison us,
And, slave to our mistrusts,
We speak to hide what we would like to say,
Lord, save us from ourselves.

Because our pleasures gladden us,
But, selfish in our delights,
We fail to offer them to You,
Lord, save us from ourselves.

How dreary for You, Lord,
Should we fail to bring You laughter,

Strong in our faith,
Relaxed within Your will,
Courageous in our thoughts,
Thankful in our joys.

How dreary, indeed,
If tears were our only alms,
Our sorrows our only worship.

That You may be spared so bleak a blasphemy,
Lord, save us from ourselves, and unite us all in You.

10 ‖ Of Discipline

Blessed Trinity, One God,
Creator of pure discipline
Increase our readiness to serve You.

Lord,
When our thoughts begin to relate
How dull a virtue patience is,
How unsatisfying,
How miserably to be endured,
Increase our readiness to serve You.

If You would ask us,
We should gladly perform
All manner of wonders for You.
Increase our readiness to serve You.

Didn't You feel impatience, Lord?
That day You frightened Your Mother,
And stayed behind in the temple,
Eager to be about Your Father's business?
You too, with hand to God,

And heart to Holy Spirit,
Were asked to wait
For eighteen years.
Increase our readiness to serve You.

But we, who are no longer young,
And still are asked to wait,
We tell ourselves
We fail to find Your help.
Is it possible, Lord,
That the name of this failure
Is Encounter?
And the nature of meaning
Is the lesson learned in waiting?
Increase our readiness to serve You.

11 ‖ Of Humility

Holy Trinity, One God,
Companion to our mirth,
Teach us to rejoice in humility.

Lord,
We give our admiration,
Flawed with envy,
To all the arts surrounding us with meaning.
We dream, for a moment,
Life is otherwise
And we the artists who make meaning clear.
Lord, teach us to rejoice in humility.

Lord,
We would forget
That we are the jugglers who drop the balls,

The actors who fail their lines,
The painters who crowd their compositions,
The writers who use unneeded words,
The dancers who miss steps,
The supplicants who offer no thanks.
Lord, teach us to rejoice in humility.

And so it is, Lord,
That on a winter's Sunday morning
We hear, as for the first time,
"Singing with grace in your hearts."
And we know that ours are not the voices
Of which heavenly choirs are made.
Lord, teach us to rejoice in humility.

But we might,
With an instant's insight,
Adore You
Through laughter at ourselves.

Lord, that this may happen,
Teach us to rejoice in humility.

12 ‖ Of Asking and Receiving

Father, Son, and Holy Spirit,
Man's Destiny, One God,
Sustain our faith.

Knowing that You love us,
How dare we ask for more?
Lord, we believe; help, now, our unbelief.

Or is it less we ask for?
We ask for things of common use,

Or things of beauty;
Or a business success,
Or victory in a game.
We plead for happiness,
And with the absolution of our sins
To be let off their consequences.
Lord, we believe; help, now, our unbelief.

If the world knows us not, because it knows You not,
Still, we know the world,
And rush out to embrace it.
Our prayers do not seem wrong to us,
For You came that we might have life more abundantly.
But You ask that we draw the picture differently:
You ask that our wants be sketched on the far horizon,
And in the foreground
Our encounter with You
Be drawn face to Face.
Lord, we believe; help, now, our unbelief.

Lord,
We grow uneasy.
You ask that we come to this abundance through You.
It was so simple
To ask all things of You.
And when You ask of us,
We feel abandoned,
And cannot understand
How, feeling abandoned,
We are yet closer to You.
Something has happened we do not know the name of.
Lord, we believe; help, now, our unbelief.

13 || Of Efforts

The beatitudes: Blessed are the poor in spirit; and those who hunger and thirst for right; the gentle and the merciful; those whose hearts are pure; the sorrowful; the peacemakers, and those who will suffer to see right prevail.

Father, Son, Holy Spirit,
Transcendent certainty, One God,
Fill our prayers with meaning.

Lord,
Let our thoughts express
A modesty of spirit,
Humility of mind.
Bless our efforts, Lord.

Let us be armed
With eagerness to know the truth of Your love
For sinners and those sinned against.
Bless our efforts, Lord.

Let us forsake all hasty judgment
That our hearts may touch Your grace.
Bless our efforts, Lord.

Let us create the warmth of peace within ourselves,
Create it with friends, with strangers,
With those we envy,
Those we pity, too.
Bless our efforts, Lord.

Let us see mourning not as sorrow
But as the courage of our faith.
Bless our efforts, Lord.

Knowing we cannot build a society
Relevant to Your purposes
Except we start with ourselves,
Release us, Lord, from all procrastination,
That Your joyous freedom
May surge through us
And spill upon mankind.
Bless our efforts, Lord.

PART II

OF THE SOCIETY
IN WHICH WE LIVE

14 ‖ Of Space

Uncreated Trinity
Encountered throughout history, One God,
Relate us to Your universe.

Lord,
Among the company of heaven
Is a man who wrote
Of his fire-filled revelations
So plainly for his audience,
But so obscurely for us,
That to learn of Your truth,
We turn to the fire-filled, lucid symbol
$E = mc^2$.
Lord, relate us to Your universe.

And we accept as fact
That space is occupied by time,
And what we thought were two
Exist as one.
Released from the gravity-hold of ignorance
We soar upon abstraction,
Experience the finite curve,
And leave behind us ancient revelation,
Except for
A and Ω
Lord, relate us to Your universe.

Revelation's beasts with eyes in front and back
We do not understand;
But pound-thrust of energy we witness.
Jasper and emerald thrones
Have no meaning for us,
But solid-fuel propulsion even our children know.
A sea of crystal may once have been,
But a missile's peroxide frost is visible.
Lord, relate us to Your universe.

Slowly this missile rises,
Gathers speed,
And hurls into space
A man.
We know he lives
Adrift beyond our sight,
And eats,
And thinks,
And experiments,
And remembers.
We know all this because we watch a screen
And see the pictured rhythm of man's heart,
And hear it beat.
And thus related to Your universe
We pray,
Lord, relate us to Your purpose, too.

15 ‖ Of Talents

Gracious Trinity, One God,
Beneficent in gifts,
Keep us mindful of Your grace.

Lord,
Whether our talents be
To orbit among the stars,
Or pray in cloistered cell,
Keep us mindful of Your grace.

Lord,
Whether our talents make
The large decisions which are peace or war,
Or the meaningful choices
That help a child to grow.
Keep us mindful of Your grace.

Lord,
Whether our talents move
Toward the threshold of the undiscovered,
Or the door of the familiar,
Keep us mindful of Your grace.

Wherever our talents take us,
It is by Your grace alone
That we learn to love without dissimulation,
Rejoice with those who rejoice,
Weep with those who weep.
Wherever our talents take us,
It is by Your grace alone
That we cheerfully journey
To Your kingdom within us.

And so that we may one day realize
These talents are not ours but gifts from You,
Lord, keep us mindful of Your grace.

16 ‖ Of the Kingdom Within

O Mystery without origin or end,
O Blessed Trinity, One God,
Have mercy upon us.

That dreadful night, that season of the dark
When savage man, deserted by the sun,
Snatched at the trees and tore them from the ground,
With rites of death to bring spring's bright return,

That bleak winter of man's mind,
When all the world,
The stars, the moon, the fields, the hills, the seas,
The floods, the storms, the noise of nature
Made a thousand gods,

That time of futile sacrifice dissolved
Into Perpetual Light
When You were born.
Lord, lead us to the Kingdom of God within.

And yet,
Today we seek those thousand gods again.
We turn our backs upon Your blinding light,
And use our brains to rearrange the world,
In primitive belief that new research,
Worshipped as though it were a golden bough,
Will save us from the need to change ourselves.
Lord, lead us to the Kingdom of God within.

We do not wish to change ourselves at all.
Our thralldom to our egos suits us well.
Preserved and strengthened by our cowardice,
Our egos teach us how we may avoid
The lonely freedom of Your discipline.
Lord, lead us to the Kingdom of God within.

Eternity, unsought, untouched, unloved,
Stretches around us, while we try to run
Into some new dimension, made by man,
Of captured particles from outer space.
Civilization has produced a bomb
Whose chain reaction fulfills ancient dreams,
And brings the power of solar energy
To man's command. Our destiny is clear:
Either we engage You one by one,
Or blow ourselves into a pagan sun.
Lord, lead us to the Kingdom of God within.

O Christ, this gift of Kingdom
God gave us with Your birth,
We pray to find it whole
And not in ruins,
Destroyed as by a child,
Impetuously,
To find it as a fortress
From which the soul,
The mind, the body,
Set forth to do Your will.
Lord, lead us to the Kingdom of God within.

17 ‖ Of Current Superstition

Profound, Eternal Godhead,
Abundant source of All,
Our Trinity, Our God,
Enlighten us.

Lord,
In a world
Where "sins and wickedness"

Are nothing but old-fashioned words,
How do we ever get to know
Ourselves?
Lord, enlighten us.

In a time
When everything has names
From the atoms in our bones
To those in Jupiter,
And these names are thought to be answers,
How do we avoid
Moral ignorance?
Lord, enlighten us.

In a life
Where crimes vanish in statistics,
Our conscience satisfied the counting has been done;
Where ethics vanish in noble codes,
Our conscience satisfied the phrasing has been done;
Where realities vanish in colored charts,
Our conscience satisfied the picture has been done;
Where learned superstition
Betrays us constantly,
In such a life, O Lord,
How shall we find You?
Lord, enlighten us.

How do we leave all this persuasive superficiality,
And go in search of You?
Lord, enlighten us.

Against this massive
Fantasy of facts
How do we bear the witness
You have asked of us?
Lord, enlighten us.

Unfashionable or not,
We do confess our sins
In knowledge of
Your forgiveness.
And let this be our witness:
Because we are repentent, not remorseful,
We lose our guilt, and with it ourselves in You.
We have Your joy
To strengthen us
To fight off complacency,
To resist the line of least resistance,
To use the tools that men devise,
That we may do Your will,
And free the mystic process of Your love
So all things truly come of You, O Lord.
We have Your joy,
And of Your own, we shall give back to You.
Lord, that we may so serve You, we pray You to enlighten us.

18 || Of Luxury

O Splendid Majesty,
Most noble Trinity, One God,
Enrich our spirit.

Dear Lord,
Let us face You,
And plead humility
To ask the daylight questions prompted by
The dusk.
Lord, enrich our spirit.

How live
This ample life
And not love luxury?
Be ravished by possessions that
Delight?
Lord, enrich our spirit.

How use,
Without flushed pride,
The cars, the food, the wine,
The pleasures of this Caesar's world
Of ours?
Lord, enrich our spirit.

How know,
And not be charmed,
Our wants all gratified
In substance and in atmosphere
Alike?
Lord, enrich our spirit.

We know we must give something of ourselves
To what we own:
Our furs, our jewels, our homes filled with devices
Beyond the hopes and dreams of ancient kings.

And we are troubled,
Kneeling before Your Cross,
Unable to decide
How much of ourselves
Is here with You,
And how much left behind
With some lovely
Treasured object.
Lord, enrich our spirit.

O God, in candor
We cannot deny
Our strong desire
To stay just as we are.

Deliver us, therefore,
By Your great love,
From bringing to You
Innocently glad,
A thing-filled emptiness
Of soul.
Lord, enrich our spirit.

19 ‖ Of Equality

Eternal Trinity,
Hope of mankind, One God,
Unite us in Your love.

Now are the sins of our fathers
On our heads; these sins
Rise among us
And parade
As prejudice, divisions, hate, fear, rebellion, and revenge,
And also, Lord,
As the color of our skins, light or dark.
Lord, give us wisdom.

If we are to know what to pray for, Lord,
If we are to bring the real problem
To You,
We must begin
By discarding the symbol of color
As of no consequence.

For it is not by color
That we are made in Your image,
But by our capacity for love.
Lord, give us wisdom.

Omnipresent God,
You, who know this earth, these hearts of ours,
What is it that divides within itself
A group all of one color, one faith, one culture?
Is it the refusal to look within ourselves,
And analyze our sins, flaws, and neuroses?
Does jealousy afflict only those of one faith, and not another?
Does felt inferiority know black from white?
Does the drive for superiority know north from south?
Does the traumatic sex experience know mother from child?
And the myths
Swarming in our unconscious,
And rising to our fantasies and dreams,
Can they distinguish the identity
Of their host?
But You know us, Lord,
As You know love from hate,
You know us all.
Lord, give us wisdom.

How discouraging it is to learn
That rather than achieve
Equality through self-correction,
We project our dissatisfactions
Onto men and circumstance.
Our capacity for love dries up.
We hide our hate and fear with paper
Printed with the laws of human rights.
Lord, before it is too late, teach us to revive
Our capacity for love.

20 ‖ Of Patriotism

Blessed Trinity, One God,
Creator of all that is,
Grant us peace.

Lord, what is it
You have tried to teach us
Through our love
For our native land?
Lord, grant us peace.

Even as we pray
For the peace, prosperity, and enlightenment
Of our country,
We know other people
Do the same
For the country they love.
Lord, grant us peace.

We find it so enjoyable to think of our country
As its mountains, or its plains, or
The sounds of the surf beating on its shores,
Or the sounds of its traffic in the cities,
Or its orchards and its farms,
Its range-lands,
Its flowers, its animals, its people.
Lord, grant us peace.

It is a long time, Lord,
Before we realize
A nation is its past
Expressed
In its present way of life.
The good and the bad of the past are here,
The glory and the failure,
The strength and the weakness,

The right choices and the wrong choices,
All are here
To be preserved
For future generations.
Lord, grant us peace.

Lord,
As we earnestly pray for peace,
The new nations of the world
Come into our thoughts,
And we feel we have foolishly been saying to them,
"Here, take our past and make it yours,
  Take our ideals,
  Bought with blood and hardship,
  And make them yours."
We ask them to take our successes
So they will never have to make our mistakes.
Lord, grant us peace.

Are we fighting the wrong battle, Lord?
You did not ask one nation absorbing many.
You asked one brotherhood,
Existing in diversity.
At Pentecost, You did not give to all people
The understanding of one language;
You gave to Your apostles
The gift of tongues
That they might speak to peoples in their own languages.
Lord, let us remember this.
Let us remember
When we feed the hungry,
Cloth the poor,
Heal the sick,
Extend the help that puts a weaker brother
On his own road to salvation

That he must know
His self-respect is earned,
That he must see in his experience
How freedom alone
Will keep his earnings for him.
Lord, grant us peace.

Lord, bless the country in which we live;
Lord, bless its leaders, too;
Lord, bless the motive with which we give;
Lord, bless our brotherhood in You.

21 ‖ Of the Children of God

Glory be to the Father,
Glory be to the Son,
Glory be to the Holy Spirit,
To the Blessed Trinity, One God,
All honor and glory be, for evermore.

Incarnate Joy,
Fill our hearts
With love.
Hear us, Good Lord.

Most Holy Miracle,
Fill our minds
With truth.
Hear us, Good Lord.

Word made Flesh,
Fill our souls
With peace.
Hear us, Good Lord.

Let this night
Find the hour
When all of us,
In all places,
In all faiths,
In all colors,
In all creeds,
In all diversity of language, custom, and of thought,
Know ourselves to be,
Through You,
The children of God.
Hear us, Good Lord.

22 || Of Political Persecution

The following litany is dedicated to victims
of religious and political persecution, present or past.

O Blessed Trinity, One God,
Host to all our sorrows,
Have mercy upon us.

This bloody century saturates our lives,
And sickens us with our inadequacy
When we see piles of nameless dead, our brothers.
Lord, have mercy upon us.

Appalled, we feel our very being numbed
By tragedy we cannot comprehend;
Where were we, when this lust of death began?
Lord, have mercy upon us.

How slow we were to realize, to know
That dedicated hatred fills some hearts.
Oh, we confess to sudden wrath,

Or even the corroding sin
Of years of dislike
For one person or another.
But nothing in our experience prepared us for
This plundering of dignity from death,
This starving, beating, killing millions
Of people
Like ourselves.
Lord, have mercy upon us.

What evil had these victims done, O Lord?
Surely their crime was hope to know the best,
A love of freedom, love of field and town,
And by Your grace, a love of man for man.
Lord, have mercy upon us.

To deliver us, to give us all Your love
You stretched Yourself in death upon the Cross.
What agony of spirit, Yours and ours,
That mankind has not yet delivered You!
Lord, have mercy upon us.

Unfit for love, we will not search our hearts,
Fearing to find that we have rationalized
Our indignation to indifference.
Lord, have mercy upon us.

O Christ,
Receive these martyred souls
In Paradise.

O Christ,
Engrave their purpose
In our lives.

Lord, have mercy upon us.
Christ, have mercy upon us.
Lord, have mercy upon us.

23 ‖ Of Brutality

The following litany is dedicated to the memory of Anne Frank,
Emmet Till, and all children who meet death by violence,
whether at the hands of disturbed parents or strangers.

God, Son, Holy Spirit,
Sacred Trinity, One God,
Teach us to be born again.

The naked brutality
Which slaughters
Children
Kills conscience, too.
Lord, teach us to be born again.

What can we bring to You
This day
Except a haunted horror
Of ourselves
For living in the company
Of evil men?
Lord, teach us to be born again.

When innocence lies murdered
Guilt touches all of us.
Lord, teach us to be born again.

Depressed, we ask where is Your Joy?
Helpless, we ask where is Your Strength?
Sickened, we ask where is Your Health?
Depraved, we ask where is Your Saving Grace?
At war within ourselves, we ask
Where is Your Peace?
Lord, teach us to be born again.

O Christ
Receive these children
To Your heart
For evermore.

O Christ
Release our hatred
Into love,
So that we may know
Our differences of faith,
Of color,
And of temperament
A source of grace,
A way to come to You.
Lord, teach us to be born again.

24 ‖ Of One Church

God the Father,
God the Son,
God the Holy Spirit,
Blessed One in Three,
Grant us brotherhood.

Lord, so that we may not be afraid
To make friends with strangers,
And accept the different with an open mind,
Grant us faith.

Lord, so that we may know each man,
Each woman, each child
To be with us joint heirs through Christ
To all eternity,
Grant us love.

Lord, so that we may live the witness
Of Your desire,
Not ours,
Grant us obedience.

Lord, so that we may build One Church
Of Your creation,
Not ours,
Grant us humility.

25 ‖ Of All Sorts and Conditions of Men

O Blessed Trinity, One God,
Eternal friend to man,
Inspire us with Your love.

That there are men who hunger for warm rice,
Or milk, or meat, or cheese,
Or even the crumbs our dogs ignore,
Lord, help us to remember.

That there are men who hunger for Your grace,
And search their minds and hearts for words of prayer,
Who, having Your love, yet fail to find its presence,
Lord, help us to remember.

That there are men who hunger to be free,
To go where they please, or stay upon their land,
Or even to think, to laugh, to plan, to hope,
Lord, help us to remember.

That there are men who thirst to know the truth,
And have at hand some small, dry cup of lies
Provided them by cynical, evil leaders,
Lord, help us to remember.

That there are men who thirst to use themselves
In surging performance of all they have learned from life,
But are held back by the jealousy of their contemporaries,
Lord, help us to remember.

That there are men who thirst to create love
In loveless circumstance of slum,
Or homeless circumstance of compound,
Lord, help us to remember.

That there are men who call their neighbor stranger,
Reject the world, and dwell within suspicion
In ignorant agony of their need for You,
Lord, help us to remember.

That there are men who, foreign to Your Church,
Still seek You in the reaches of their hearts
And would come forth if they were gently asked,
Lord, help us to remember.

That there are men who, alien to themselves,
Become uneasy friends with fear,
Yet might with a moment's grace rejoice in knowledge of Your
       love,
Lord, help us to remember.

That there are men naked to weather,
Helpless before torture,
Sick with disease and with loneliness,
That there are men prisoner to the walls of tyrants,
And prisoner to the walls of indifference,
That in the least of these Your kingdom waits our love,
Lord, help us to remember.

Grant to us, O God,
A total stewardship of self,
Possessions, and endeavor,
By hour, and by day,
By moment, and by night,
For the sake of Him who came among us
To serve us all.

Lord, keep us in the faith which sustains
All sorts and conditions of men.

26 ‖ Of Dedication

Creator, Redeemer, Sanctifier,
Sacred Mystery, One God,
Help us to be a constructive part of the world in which we live.

That we may urge
Our hearts and minds
To love of excellence
In every routine task we must perform,
Lord, grant us dedication.

That we may learn
These tasks are mother
To life's divine significance,
Lord, grant us dedication.

That we may understand and know,
As we know breath, and bone, and pain, and joy,
A duty half performed
Is time with You forever lost,
Lord, grant us dedication.

That we may portion
Gladness to each day,
Accepting, not seeking,
Giving, not asking,
Embracing, not rejecting,
Waiting, not running,
Surrendering, not commanding,
Until lost in Your companionship
We find a loving friendship with each other;
That all of this may be,
Lord, grant us dedication.

PART III

THE SEVEN AGES OF MAN

27 ‖ Childhood

Holy Trinity, One God,
Known to us in prayer,
Keep us to Yourself.

Day-star of our souls
Please guide us.
Night-sun of our thoughts
Give light.
Lord, keep us to Yourself.

Shepherd of the Way
Keep watch.
Dear Lamb of God
Redeem us.
Lord, keep us to Yourself.

Majesty and Might
Protect us.
Love and Mercy
Be our faith.
Lord, keep us to Yourself.

28 ‖ School

Holy Trinity, One God,
Fixed in all that is changeable,
Help us keep things straight.

Lord,
Why do we have to learn so much
That we don't care about?
To sit still,
To study,
To keep at a thing until we have it through our heads?
Lord, help us keep things straight.

Lord,
So much of this isn't fun.
And we try to get by and not learn it,
And tests find out what we have not done.
We can't lie
And keep things secret
The way we could when we were little.
Lord, help us keep things straight.

Lord,
The teacher said
We never were supposed to lie, and
Make ourselves
Flimsy imitations of people
Who collapse at the first challenge.
We do not want to be like them.
Lord, help us keep things straight.

Lord,
If we can't have anything
Unless we work for it,
We'll need Your help.
Help us remember
That when we have really learned a thing,
Or know how to do something,
Whether it is history,
Or arithmetic,
Or drawing,

Or singing,
Or high-jumping,
Or pinch-hitting,
Or swimming,
Or whatever,
When we really know it,
And can do it,
Nobody can take it away from us.
To have skill
Is not the same as having a toy
That can get broken,
Or be put up on a shelf.
And yet, in a way,
This frightens us,
Because we cannot tell
Whether to learn
Will make us different from what we are
Or make us more ourselves.
Lord, help us keep things straight.

29 ‖ Youth

Everlasting Trinity,
Creator of all energy, One God,
Keep us eager for the truth.

Lord,
When we were children,
People seemed so big, so strong, so old,
We learned to think of You
As a Man older than anybody,
As a Man who would be good to us,
If we were good,

As a Man who would punish us,
If we were bad.
Be with us, Lord, in our confession.

We learned other things, too, Lord:
We watched people quarrel,
And one would swear,
And one would cry,
And so much that was unfair would happen,
And we wanted to make things right.
We had learned a feeling we didn't know about.
But now, we think we had learned
What pity is.
Be with us, Lord, in our confession.

We feel a strangeness
In putting a name to what we know.
For if we did learn pity—
If we did find out
That putting ourselves in another's place
Made life less black and white,
And yet made it mean more—
If we did learn *that,*
Why then we had learned to know something
About You.
Be with us, Lord, in our confession.

For You came to make things right.
You came to take away the sins of the world,
And we must believe, therefore,
The world is what it is
Because people will not let go their sins.
And we, too, are of the people
In this world.
Be with us, Lord, in our confession.

We are people who would like to think
That sinners are those
Other than ourselves.
And so we hesitate to tell You,
That we want the experience of love without regret;
That we want the privileges
Of driving sixty miles an hour without danger to other drivers,
Of staying up late without missing anything next day,
Of passing examinations without our daily study,
Of drinking without getting sick,
Of neglecting our neighbors of different colors and beliefs
        without hurting them,
Of having our own way without spoiling anything for our
        families,
Of doing all we are told not to do without getting caught.
Yes, Lord,
We want the sins of laziness and pride
To bear the respectable names
Of virtues,
Because they are surely not as bad as the sins we read about.
Be with us, Lord, in our confession.

Yet, we know You ask more of us
Than that we live some tarnished lie of restless happiness
That has no bone of truth, no muscle of joy, no flesh of bravery,
And so we do confess our sins,
Praying for the grace of true repentance,
Free of the self-abuse of remorse.
Be with us, Lord, in our confession.

We shall make many mistakes of feeling,
In trying to learn true repentance,
In trying to know the difference
Between having our sins put away by Your forgiveness,
And yet having sin's aftermath

45

To modify, correct, and use
As the foundation
For a life of active charity.
When this happens, Lord,
Help us remember Your Mother.
How old was she when the angel came?
Fourteen? Sixteen? Thirteen?
Let us remember that she said:
"Be it unto me, according to Your word."
Lord, keep us eager for the truth.

30 ‖ Soldier

Holy Trinity, One God,
Militant on earth,
Save us.

Lord,
Drill and discipline, we hate,
And being uprooted from all we know.
And yet,
Being fast made men
Holds excitements.
Save us, Lord.

In the routine
One day is like another,
But in not knowing
Where we will end,
No planning is possible,
And all we surely have
Is today,
This moment.
Save us, Lord.

And if we try to crowd into this moment
All we know of life,
Its pleasure, its courage,
Its imperfections, too,
Know, Lord,
That we are not deserting You.
Save us, Lord.

If we are to know You,
And not think of You
As a memory of something we heard in Sunday school,
Then our meeting must take place at once.
We have no time
To learn all life's dimensions,
But only two named:
Here and now.
Save us, Lord.

31 ‖ Life's Work

Holy Trinity,
Incarnate God,
Sanctify our lives.

Lord,
We learn at the end of youth
That the realization of hope begins
With marriage and with work.
Our waiting until we are adult is ended.
Now we look ahead
To success,
And family,
And participation
In the improvement of our world.

The community of men
Makes room for us.
Lord, sanctify our lives.

But we would be less than honest
With You, Lord,
If we did not confess that our confidence
Is edged about with small uncertainties.
Is uncertainty the ground
Where faith is learned?
Lord, sanctify our lives.

And, Lord,
If our commitments
Overtake the time at our disposal
To speak with You,
Accept our love and work
As worship of You.
Lord, sanctify our lives.

32 ‖ Success and Failure

Holy Trinity, One God,
Knowledgable of the minds of men,
Help us make life worthwhile.

Lord,
A day comes
When we must face the fact
That the curve of our life sweeps downward.
If misfortune falls upon us, its signs are sudden.
But we are not thinking of the swift blows of drastic change.

We would talk with You of the day
That is like yesterday,
And also like tomorrow.
Lord, help us make life worthwhile.

Lord, the knowing that we become aware of, little by little,
The knowing that promotions are at an end
That work is almost over,
The knowing that we have given our children
All we can of wisdom, help, gifts,
The knowing that their homes may need to receive us,
The knowing that,
As we have made others happy,
We also made them unhappy,
This knowledge, Lord, we bring to You and ask
Help us make life worthwhile.

When the reflective moment comes,
Its meaning whole
And clearly felt,
When this time comes, Lord
Be close to us
For no tomorrow need be like today
Since You can transform
Our life's experience
On the instant,
And by Your grace
Restore us to life's purpose
In restoring us to You.
Lord, help us make life worthwhile.

33 || Old Age

Holy Trinity, One God,
Gateway to eternity,
Help us to Your kingdom.

Lord,
Our thoughts are as hard to communicate
As they were when we were children.
We talk,
Sometimes endlessly, we fear,
And the expressions on the faces of listeners
Show that they do not hear.
Preoccupied,
They wait to leave us.
Lord, let us meet again, in You.

But it need not be a sorrow
To find ourselves alone.
We need some time
To rearrange our memories
And discard mistaken choices,
So that what we keep
To bring to You
May be named the best we knew.
And yet,
Our losses we recall with pain.
With the ache in our bones
Comes an aching longing
To hear again a familiar laugh,
To feel the tenderness,
To share.
Lord, save us from living on memory.
You have the company of those we loved.
You share it now.

To be old is to miss those with whom we learned our sharing.
Lord, teach us how to share through You.

Still, Lord, we must not
Neglect the present.
Today may be the last we have
To enjoy
The manner in which morning sunlight comes,
And evening shadows lengthen;
To smile at friends;
To read a printed page,
Let some wisdom
We did not know before
Strike at our hearts with
Leaping recognition.
Yes!
Tonight our souls may be required of us.
Lord, let us today be learning something new.

34 || Unspecified Anxieties

Blessed Trinity, One God,
Known to us through faith,
Ease our minds.

Lord,
It sometimes seems
That of all You have tried to teach us,
The lesson of taking no thought for the morrow
Is most difficult to learn.
Lord, ease our minds.

Tomorrow comes
And finds us unprepared.
Something is wrong
In the way we go about
Being lilies of the field.
Our faith is tried,
And our thoughts wander.
Lord, ease our minds.

We have anxieties
Not born of extravagance,
Or lack of safety,
Or disappointment,
Or anything we can put a name on.
And yet,
We feel ourselves
Driven,
Incompetent,

Vexed,
Ready to quarrel, find fault,
Give up the effort
To follow You
Into the kingdom within ourselves.
Lord, ease our minds.

No, we cannot follow You.
Our time is needed
Somehow to get through the day
And be ready for tomorrow.
But, Lord,
How do we cast our cares on You?
Lord, what did You mean?
Lord, ease our minds.
Lord, grant us insight into Your teaching.

35 ‖ Divorce

Holy Trinity, One God,
Constant in devotion,
Help us work through grief to understanding.

Lord,
Death is not the worst of final moments.
The worst is to believe
That life is whole,
The choice accepted,
Today a happy part of tomorrow's coming—
The worst is to believe all these,
And then to hear the words
"You are not loved."
Lord, help us work through grief to understanding.

What happened, we ask ourselves,
When did the good so long in building
Start to decay?
Lord, in our despair,
We feel You leave us, too.
What is love
If not the day to day
Enlarging of the self by two people
Through passion, patience, memories, and work?
This cannot be done again
With someone else.
Lord, help us work through grief to understanding.

Lord,
You taught that love is selflessness,
A giving without thought of return,
A joyous expenditure of self,
Without counting cost.
But, Lord,
From the day we are born
All other lessons are at odds with Yours.
Once we are slapped into breath
The conflict of our needs with others' needs begins.
The visible needs of the cold and hungry
Are met with goods we do not even miss;
But these other needs,
The need to see nobility in imperfection,
Beauty in plainness,
Ambition in amiable, or grudging, responsibility,
Ideals in the simple effort,
The need to find cheerfulness, encouragement, help,
All this we seek to find in others,
And we evade the giving of it when we are asked.
Or, perhaps, we try some token giving
To gain for us the whole of another's being.

Science names our seeking a substitute for love: projection.
Lord, help us work through grief to understanding.

The heart is broken.
The name of a feeling
Is not the feeling itself.
That which gives, or seeks, or both,
Is still within us,
Dislodged,
And floating aimlessly,
Hurtfully.
We need You, Lord.
Help us work through grief to understanding.

36 ‖ Loneliness

Blessed Trinity,
Manifest eternity, One God,
Help us watch one hour with You.

Lord,
We say we are lonely,
That we need someone to talk to.
That we miss the companionship of those who have died,
That our days are incomplete
Because that which would complete them
Is not in them.
Lord, help us watch one hour with You.

Is all loneliness the same?
Can those who suffer physical loneliness
Give understanding to those who suffer intellectual
Loneliness?
Can the lonely who feel shut out because of race

Give love to the lonely who feel shut out
Because they do not conform?
In the end, Lord,
Are the many kinds of loneliness
One kind?
Lord, help us watch one hour with You.

Is loneliness a condition of existence
Like orbiting atoms?
It is difficult to explore this matter with You, Lord,
Because it is difficult to know
With what perfection we compare our state.
We do know
Some sudden opinion, vivid memory, spontaneous thought,
Angry departure
From those closest to us
Can open a chasm so wide
As to leave us feeling
We fall through measureless space
Alone.
Lord, help us watch one hour with You.

And yet,
We do not forsake each other,
Not always, anyway.
A bottom of despair is reached at last
Where pain itself must medicine the soul.
And here, Lord,
Here we want
The assurance of Your presence.
You that we cannot see
Nor touch,
Whose words fight with our agony
For hearing,
You we want to know, You, here at the bottom.

And here to create that knowing,
You send us to each other.
You that watch with us always
Help us thoughtfully watch with one another hour by hour.

37 ‖ Suicide Contemplated

Holy Trinity, One God,
Merciful in judgment,
Help us find You.

If You require us to
Ask ourselves
Why we dare choose the moment for
Death,
Then we shall know we dare not choose it.
Lord, teach us self-forgetfulness.

We say
Life has been unfair,
And even our friends assure us
That it has.
We have more problems
Than we know how to handle,
And everyone who knows us
Knows this is so.
Lord, teach us self-forgetfulness.

We say
We are hungry,
Or moneyless,
Or friendless,
Or that our family
Long ago

Abandoned us;
And even the stranger
We tell it to
Sees our complaints as facts.
Lord, teach us self-forgetfulness.

And so
When we would give up life,
You stay our hand,
And ask that we give up self instead.
This takes some learning, Lord,
And teachers are hard to come by.
Still, let us
Now
Put our faith in You.
We would like some fellow-students
At this school.
But, if we must learn alone,
Lord, teach us self-forgetfulness.

38 ‖ Suicide Committed

Holy Trinity, One God,
Comprehending the trials of men,
Receive our souls.

Lord,
This good-bye
Is beyond bearing.
Self-reproaches crowd the mind,
Trying to find utterance,
And we ask what happened?
Why?

Where did we fail?
Lord, help us to resolution.

Did we say too little,
Or too much?
Did we extend the helping hand
To the point of its becoming
A burden?
Or did we withhold the help needed,
Waiting to be asked for it?
Lord, help us to resolution.

How empty
All our busyness seems now,
How futile our hopes,
How hurtful
Our misjudgment.
Lord, help us.

Did we do all we could?
Was the flight of this soul
From us to You
Beyond our ability
To stop?
Lord, help us know the answer.

Lord, teach us to forget ourselves
And find You in the joy
We must learn to bring to others,
That they, in turn,
May find themselves
In You.
Lord, teach us self-forgetfulness.

39 ‖ Illness

Blessed Trinity,
Physician to the soul, One God,
Heal our infirmities.

When we look into,
Or look out from,
The face of suffering,
And find You there,
We know we have been blessed.
For it is simple
To say, "If You were good, and just, and kind,
You would not let such illness happen."
Lord, heal our infirmities.

The imperfections in the world,
The imperfections in the flesh, the mind,
The pain, Lord,
The pain that is in life,
In bone, in nerve, in personality,
All these
Are the narrow edge of experience
On which we move closer to You,
Or turn our backs and go the other way.
Lord, heal our infirmities.

We are taught that
You make our sickness bearable.
We do not think so.
We think
You give it meaning,
Make life's purpose real,
And not a gesture of the voice.
Courage is with us,
And fear.

Lord,
Let the healing be now
Or when we come into Your perfect service.
We would be whole
With You
In Paradise.
Lord, heal our infirmities.

40 ‖ Accidents

Blessed Trinity, One God,
Beyond the accidents of time,
Relieve our sudden sorrow.

Lord,
The horror of the moment
Overcomes us,
Our thoughts refuse to shape themselves,
And tears contain all we know how to say.
Lord, relieve our sudden sorrow.

What was to have been a day like any other
Is disaster.
Our love is
Defeated by tragedy,
And grief
Is too new to understand.
Lord, relieve our sudden sorrow.

Every day brings to You, Lord,
Those who leave behind them
The unprepared,
The inexperienced in loss,
And we are among this number.

Lord, let the love we held so dearly
Live again, and grow through You.
Lord, relieve our sudden sorrow.

41 ‖ Death

Holy Trinity, One God,
Destination of man's soul,
Give us grace.

Lord,
When someone we love is dead,
And we must turn away
From the grave of the body's rest
To walk alone,
Come Holy Spirit, and fill us with Your grace.

When the terrain has hills we did not see before,
And the days are longer than we knew,
The nights less restful than we remembered,
Oh, when we miss the strength that they supplied,
Come Holy Spirit, and fill us with Your grace.

And when at the last
We, too, relinquish breath,
In one swift moment
Leaving
The life we knew
For the life that is to be,
Come Holy Spirit, and fill us with Your grace.

PART V

THE SEVEN CAPITAL SINS

42 ‖ The Capital Sin of Pride

Sublime and thoughtful Trinity,
Manifest in humility, One God,
Absolve us from the sin of pride.

How brilliant a sin is pride when seen in others,
How little recognized within ourselves.
It veils itself in arrogance of speech;
It builds support for a rigid frame of mind;
It multiplies excuses for our errors;
It dissipates our prayers in stylized chatter;
It chains us to the devil's inclinations;
And though these chains be light and long,
They keep us from the freedom
Of Your love.
Lord, absolve us from the sin of pride.

Yet, puppet-like we sit upon pride's lap,
Giving the name of grief to discontent,
Giving the name of wit to impudence,
Giving the name of righteousness to fear,
Giving the name of justice to desire,
Giving the name of courage to haste,
Giving the name of wisdom to hesitation,
Giving the name of truth to information.
And we feel that when pride speaks through us,
No man may call us fool.
Lord, absolve us from the sin of pride.

What a progenitor of sin pride is!
By the simple means of keeping the mirror of self
Constantly before our eyes,
Pride turns the trivial into cause for wrath,
Makes of a feast an occasion for gluttony,
Knifes joy apart with the sharp edge of envy,
Yields love to boredom's lust,
Thwarts satisfaction until it becomes greed.
And finally pride refuses
The grace You would give us today,
And lets us name sloth
Hope for perfection in tomorrow.
Lord, absolve us from the sin of pride.

God,
Pride is the sin
That was traitor to an angel.
We, who are less than angels,
Ask Your help in discerning
This wily sin
That travels with us,
Now by one name, now by another.
Lord, absolve us from the sin of pride.

43 ‖ The Capital Sin of Wrath

Patient Trinity, One God,
Source of our salvation,
Have mercy upon us.

Lord,
We know
Wrath is a cork
That can be blown

By frustration.
Then clashes, words, wreckage,
Impulsive indulgence
In anything at hand
Spill from us
In senseless energy.
Lord, help us know what our problems truly are.

The wrathful reaction
Is quicker almost
Than the perception of its cause.
The muscles tense;
The heart beats rapidly;
The neck bulges;
The mouth is drawn;
The mind is filled
With the blood of rage,
And there is no room for thought.
The lash of hand, or tongue,
Explodes.
Lord, help us know what our problems truly are.

Another time,
Wrath may be slow.
We carry on
Internal arguments
On the lack of fairness in our lives,
While others find a fairness, undeserved;
We say the impossible is asked of us,
While others could do more if they would.
The silent dialogue
Goes on
In endless foolishness.
Lord, help us know what our problems truly are.

Lord,
What causes us
To choose the sin of wrath
As a means of getting what we want,
Or as a means of
Getting even with life?
Is fear the other name of wrath?
Or is it utter lovelessness!
No love at all,
No knowledge of love's meaning,
No love of self, of others, or of You.
What an assassination of the soul it is
When hatred is the weapon,
Wrath the method.
Lord, save us from the sin of wrath.

44 || The Capital Sin of Envy

Creator,
Redeemer,
Sanctifier,
Healing Trinity, One God,
Hear our prayers.

Lord,
We never feel so sick
As when our
Hurts, hatreds, and rejections
Take refuge in the sin
Of envy.
Lord, teach us wholesome self-love.

Safe within envy's refuge,
We build the

Invisible prison of possessiveness
For family,
Friend,
For all we would love
If we knew how to love.
Lord, teach us wholesome self-love.

If we are to love our neighbors as ourselves
We have great need to learn to love ourselves,
For when all else fails,
We take the self-hatred of envy
Into compulsive self-justification,
Into false causes, equivocal good works,
Into lynch-mobs,
Into the self-deluded storm-troops
Who make a habit of mass-murder.
Lord,
We believe
Envy cannot survive
The open heart, the helping hand.
Lord, save us from identifying ourselves with envy.
Lord, teach us wholesome self-love.

45 ‖ The Capital Sin of Covetousness

Generous Trinity, One God,
Known to us through faith,
Teach us contentment.

Lord,
What is the source of discontent
That makes us greedy?
Oh, if we had been deprived when we were young,

If we had much to compensate for,
Why then some greediness is understood.
Lord, teach us contentment.

But, Lord,
Simply to accumulate
Money,
And things,
And marriages,
As though the boundaries of satisfaction
Could be owned,
Enclosing an estate of happiness,
Seems so futile a sin
No urge to greediness should ever
Prevent our seeing it.
Lord, teach us contentment.

And then there is another greediness,
Turning our love to selfishness,
Lest being generous of heart
We should be hurt.
And when this happens,
Lord,
What should have been
The silent joy of sympathy
Becomes a mirthless sob
Of wretchedness.
Lord,
Why is it
When You give us the road to heaven
We study the map of hell?
Lord, teach us contentment.

46 ‖ The Capital Sin of Sloth

Dynamic Trinity, One God,
Known through action,
Help us fill today with meaning.

Lord,
We see men sitting on curbstones
Their heads on their knees,
Or lying asleep in alleyways;
We see dirty shacks,
With dirty children playing about,
We see all manner
Of forlornness,
And some of it is due to circumstance,
But some of it began with choice.
And we ask ourselves if we are making choices
Whose end will be
Conspicuous as these.
Lord, help us fill today with meaning.

Are we ever so tired we cannot do what we should,
But so enterprising we can do what we want to?
What leads us in so many thoughtless ways
To choose unplanned neglect
Of homes and families,
Jobs, ourselves,
That we may have the time
To escape into diversions
Which reward us by demanding nothing of us.
Lord, help us fill today with meaning.

We wish we did not have to learn
What a subtle sin sloth is.
By urging "Choose this;
Neglect that,"

It carries the full weight of
Social approval,
Of community-mindedness.
And who will ever know
The higgledy-piggledy mess
Hid in the closet?
Sloth wears two names,
Depending on our weakness:
The one is idleness,
The other busyness.
We feel discouraged and do not know why.
Lord, save us from this self-deception.
Lord, help us know the difference
Between the meaningful and the meaningless.
Lord, help us fill today with meaning.

47 ‖ The Capital Sin of Gluttony

Sustaining Trinity, One God,
Found through bread and wine,
Teach us courage.

Lord,
We swallow our disappointments
With too much food,
Or too much alcohol,
And what was once a pleasure
Becomes a vice,
A poisoned medicine,
A sickness,
A sin.
Teach us courage, Lord.

We find this putting something into our mouths
A comforting substitute
For sorting out
Our faults and errors;
And it is infinitely easier
To face a glass
Or plate
Than the rearrangement of our hopes,
The acceptance of our situations.
Teach us courage, Lord.

Oh, Lord,
The cause of all of this lies deep,
And change of ourselves is a wrench that frightens us.
Still,
We know from You that
If we could say "The past is gone,
Today is all we have to meet, to conquer,"
Our desperation would retreat to moderation,
Our sins remit to pleasures once again,
Our hopes be filled with joy.
Lord, teach us courage.

48 ‖ The Capital Sin of Lust

Blessed Trinity,
Object of our devotion, One God,
Teach us how to love.

This lust,
This panic of the flesh,
This shiver of desire,
This, too, O Lord,

We bring to You
And ask,
Lord, how do we make impulse part of love?

Possessor and possessed
We come to You and ask,
Lord, how do we lose ourselves in love of You?

Urged by a strength
We did not know we had,
Yet weak in the fear
That time will pass us by,
Lord, how do we turn the moment to true love?

Lord, teach us love,
Now while our flesh is warm,
Our muscles firm,
Our minds alert,
Our hearts generous.
Lord, have mercy upon us.

We would learn the lesson, Lord,
By choice,
And not through the helplessness of age.
Christ, have mercy upon us.

Yours is a love of affirmation, Lord,
And not denial.
Thus we would love,
Thus know ourselves through You.
Lord, have mercy upon us.

PART VI

OF LOVE

49 ‖ Of Faith

I may speak in tongues of men or of angels, but if I am without
love, I am a sounding gong or a clanging cymbal. I may have
the gift of prophecy, and know every hidden truth; I may have
faith strong enough to move mountains; but if I have no love,
I am nothing.   v. 1-2.

Lord,
When do we have faith
Without love?
Is it when, exasperated by circumstance,
We curse friend and enemy alike?
Is it when we dare some spite
To save our pride?
Or when we perform as cold duty
What should be instant generosity?
Lord, give us an answer we can understand.

We bring our worldly cares to You
Each Sunday
And hope for a Monday answer.
Monday is impersonal, competitive, immediate.
We have faith on a holy morning.
Where has it gone by a mid-week's evening?
Our faith feels firm,
But in the days between our worship of You
Anxieties accumulate.

We would not forgo
The beauty
Of Sunday's poignant prose,
But we fail, somehow,
To realize it in our living.
Lord ,why is this so?
Lord, give us an answer we can understand.

50 ‖ Of Hope

I may dole out all I possess, or even give my body to be burnt,
but if I have no love, I am none the better.
Love is patient; love is kind and envies no one. Love is never
boastful, nor conceited, nor rude; never selfish, not quick to take
offence. Love keeps no score of wrongs; does not gloat over other
men's sins, but delights in the truth. There is nothing love cannot face; there is no limit to its faith, its hope, and its endurance.

v. 3-7.

Lord,
When do we strike love from our hopes?
Is it when we hope for more possessions?
For recognition?
For happiness?
Is it in this hoping for ourselves alone?
Is it in trying to realize our hopes through our children?
Lord, is it when we take
So large and patient a thing
As hope
And make of it small urgencies?
Lord, give us an answer we can understand.

We are what we hope for, aren't we, Lord.
If our hopes are small, we are small.
More, we defend our smallness
By praying for our hopes to be realized
In terms and goods the world can understand—
That we can understand.
If this is not what You want of us,
How do we achieve Godly hope
In a godless society?
Lord, help us know the answer.

51 ‖ Of Love Questioned

Love will never come to an end. Are there prophets? their work
will be over. Are there tongues of ecstasy? they will cease. Is
there knowledge? it will vanish away; for our knowledge and
our prophecy alike are partial, and the partial vanishes when
the wholeness comes.   v. 8-10.

Lord,
What is the nature of love,
That it is so difficult to learn?
What is the nature of the wholeness
Which has no end?
When the desperate question
Gets a quiet answer
We do not comprehend it.
We who are in part,
We fear this vanishing away.
Lord, give us an answer we can understand.

You have answered our prayer for certainty
By offering us love.

We must stretch the heart and mind
In unself-seeking love of all life offers.
We must endure the failing prophecies we wish to heed,
The silencing of voices we wish to follow;
The vanishing of knowledge we wish to hold as truth.
The lasting question posed in all times, all places
Receives relative answers
Learned in the situation.
Lord,
Is it Your gift of love
Which makes Your gift of
Free will
Bearable?
Lord, accept and enlarge our understanding.

52 ‖ Of Love Perceived

When I was a child, my speech, my outlook, and my thoughts
were all childish. When I grew up, I had finished with childish
things. Now we see only puzzling reflections in a mirror, but
then shall we see face to face. My knowledge now is partial;
then it will be whole, like God's knowledge of me. In a word,
there are three things that last forever: faith, hope, and love;
but the greatest of them all is love.   v. 11-13.

Lord,
The finishing with childish things
Is the work of a lifetime.
Long before we have done with
Our whims, our selfishness, our tiny hopes,
We come to You and ask
That the mirror be abolished
So that we may see You
Plainly and clearly.

We do not know what we ask,
Do we, Lord?
Lord, help us use our gift of love.

We, who would serve You,
Fail to realize
This service begins
With putting away the essence of ourselves,
Only to get it back again,
Tempered and shaped
For Your use.
This is a lonely moment, Lord.
Don't leave us.
Lord, help us use our gift of love.

PART VII

ASPECTS OF TRUTH

53 || Of Fasting

Father,
Son,
Holy Spirit,
Source of eternal truth, One God,
Teach us who we are.

At times when our prayers,
Sincerely offered,
Stop with the known, and those who are dear to mind,
Lord, help us pray for the unremembered.

At times when our faith,
But half committed,
Bewilders us with its inadequacy,
Lord, help us pledge our time and thoughts to You.

At times when our tears,
Helplessly shed,
Mark hours when we know not how to find You,
Lord, help us perfect our strength in weakness.

At times when our thirsts,
Frivolously indulged,
Remain to urge that we seek Your Redeeming Cup,
Lord, help us repent our sins.

And then, when our death,
So long, so soon, in coming,
Seeks out the meeting we cannot escape,
Lord, help us accept the moment without regret.

Before we die,
We pray our witness serves You.
We pray that once we may have shunned hypocrisy
And secretly offered our will in Lenten fast,
Thus learning who we are:
Your child, Your messenger, Your friend.
We pray, at the last,
Our commended spirit may
Rest in Your hands, absolved of all distress.

Lord, have mercy upon us.
Christ, have mercy upon us.
Lord, have mercy upon us.

54 ‖ Of Action

Holy Trinity, One God,
Teacher of mankind,
Let us learn from You.

We have so little learning,
And such parochial judgment,
That any popularity of our opinions
Can persuade us
We have dispatched final truth.
Lord, let us learn from You.

You knew, Lord, when You rode into the town,
And heard the welcoming shouts of the crowd,
And watched the palms flung in Your path,
You knew that road was not to truth
Except through martyrdom.
Lord, let us learn from You.

And this You do not ask of us,
Or rarely so,
And we are glad of Your mercy,
For few of us are of the stuff
That makes martyrs.
Lord, let us learn from You.

Yes, Lord, let us learn a humble lesson.
Your truth becomes known
Not as history memorized from long ago
But as an action taken by us today.
Lord, let our actions serve to spread Your word.

55 ‖ Of Self-Forgiveness

Loving One in Three,
Trinity tested through tragedy, One God,
Have mercy upon us.

Lord,
When we are cowards
Who cannot share the travail of Your Cross,
You ask God
To forgive us.
Lord, teach us to forgive ourselves.

Lord,
When we are idlers
Who gamble away life's dear resource of time,
You ask God
To forgive us.
Lord, teach us to forgive ourselves.

Lord,
When we are bigots
Who cherish false opinion as the truth,
You ask God
To forgive us.
Lord, teach us to forgive ourselves.

Lord,
When we are grumblers
Who magnify resentments into wrongs,
You ask God
To forgive us.
Lord, teach us to forgive ourselves.

Lord,
When we are hedonists
Who cheat our pleasures of their innocence,
You ask God
To forgive us.
Lord, teach us to forgive ourselves.

Lord,
When we are cynics
Who ambush faith, and war upon God's grace,
You ask God
To forgive us.
Lord, teach us to forgive ourselves.

Lord,
When we are fools
Who must be suffered gladly,
You ask God
To forgive us.
Lord, teach us to forgive ourselves.

Unless, Lord,
We forgive ourselves,
God's great forgiveness
Becomes an affront
So unendurable we seek all means
Whereby we may escape its claim.
But if once we may reach
Behind our masks,
Replace our subterfuge
With loving courage,
The promise of God's grace awaits us.
Lord, teach us to forgive ourselves.

56 ‖ Of Resurrection

Holy Trinity, One God,
Known through Resurrection,
Accept our worship.

Lord,
We do not rise to say the creeds
As belief in something outside ourselves,
But rather to reveal
A faith within us.
Accept our worship, Lord.

For unless
We have reached
Your kingdom within our hearts,
Your Resurrection has been
For us
In vain.
Accept our worship, Lord.

Death is not so terrifying,
Nor eternal life so glorious
As to justify
Your mighty act
Save we learn how to love
Through You.
Accept our worship, Lord.

Lord,
Keep us ever mindful
Your Spirit lives
In us.
Accept our worship, Lord.

57 ‖ Of the Holy Sacrament

Holy Trinity, One God,
Known to us in the Sacrament,
Keep us in Your faith.

Lord,
You are hailed with bursts of music,
Hymns of praise and glory,
Voices raised in exultant adoration.
But, Lord,
You are also greeted
In the thankful silence
Of our hearts.
Keep us in Your faith.

You come to us in Substance
At the altar,
But, Lord,
You also come

In the grateful thoughts
Of our minds.
Keep us in Your faith.

The Sacrament
Exists within the moment, too.
In darkness we cry out to find Your help.
Pursuit in wrong directions forces us to the
Turning of ourselves around,
And there You are:
The everlasting Light.

And we are still
And know
That You are
God.

Index for Use with the Church Calendar

Following are suggestions for litanies appropriate to various days in the Church Calendar. The litany numbers are in parentheses. The reader's own judgment, however, should be the deciding factor.

ADVENT
First Sunday (2)
Second Sunday (16)
Third Sunday (17)
Fourth Sunday (18)

CHRISTMASTIDE
Christmas Eve (21)
St. Stephen's Day (22)
St. John Evangelist (4)
Holy Innocents (23)
First Sunday after Christmas (24)
Second Sunday after Christmas (6)

EPIPHANY (7)
First Sunday (8)
Second Sunday (15)
Third Sunday (9)
Fourth Sunday (10)
Fifth Sunday (11)
Sixth Sunday (12)
Septuagesima (19)
Sexagesima (32)
Quinquagesima (39)
Ash Wednesday (53)

LENT
First Sunday (49)
Second Sunday (50)
Third Sunday (51)
Fourth Sunday (52)
Passion Sunday (41)
Palm Sunday (54)
Holy Monday (36)
Holy Tuesday (37)
Holy Wednesday (26)
Maundy Thursday (57)
Good Friday (55)

OTHER DAYS
Easter (56)
Ascension (5)
Whitsunday (20)
Trinity (14)
A Saint's Day (25)
All Saints' Day (13)
Sunday next before
     Advent (1)